Mr. Alexander's
Four Steps to Love

Mr. Alexander's
Four Steps to Love

The Simple Way
to Find
Your Dream Partner

by
Alexander Stadler
with
Jennifer Worick

QUIRK BOOKS

PHILADELPHIA

Library of Congress Cataloging in Publication Number: 200309177

ISBN: 1-931686-52-1

Printed in Singapore

Typeset in Mr. Alex, Aunt Mildred, Prestige Elite

Designed by Michael Rogalski

Distributed in North America by Chronicle Books
85 Second Street
San Francisco, CA 94105

10 9 8 7 6 5 4 3 2 1

Quirk Books
215 Church Street
Philadelphia, PA 19106
www.quirkbooks.com

For Andy, of course.

CONTENTS

Mr. Alexander's Four Steps to Love:
An Introduction

MR. ALEXANDER

At a time in my life when I was trying to clean up my act and become a grown-up, the idea for this book started percolating in my head.

Until then, I thought a partner was someone you put up with. In my opinion, everyone out there was crazy, and you just chose the best-looking and most bearable partner you could find. I certainly didn't think it was possible to be with someone I adored, let alone one who liked me just as I was.

I began to ask myself questions. Why haven't I ever asked for the best thing on the menu? Why shouldn't I ask for someone who likes me the way I am? And, if I had a dream partner, who would that person be?

I realized I might not be able to control who shows up, but I could control who I asked for, so I should ask for someone good.

This book is for people who are—like I was—feeling stuck. In the pages before you, you're going to follow four simple steps: (1) make a list of the qualities you would want in an ideal partner; (2) perform a small action to make yourself feel cuter; (3) join a class, club, or group; and (4) return to your original list and take on some of those qualities. Your simple actions will create movement and change in your life!

Mr. Alexander's Four Steps to Love is a system for learning how to ask for what you want. My goal is to help you find love—possibly with somebody else, but most importantly, for yourself.

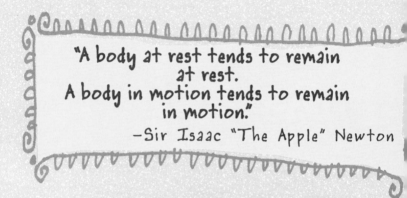

"A body at rest tends to remain
at rest.
A body in motion tends to remain
in motion."
—Sir Isaac "The Apple" Newton

"Get your freak on."
—Missy "Misdemeanor" Elliott

Why Do I Need
MR. ALEXANDER'S
FOUR STEPS TO LOVE?

I just can't meet anyone.
I've already met every-one.
I love to knit.
I don't know how to do this.
I hate the scene.
I can't find anyone who likes golf.

What Can MR. ALEXANDER'S FOUR STEPS TO LOVE Do for Me?

Mr. Alexander's
Four Steps to Love
is more fun
than a car full of clowns!

clown →

Mr. Alexander's
Four Steps to Love
will help you replace
vague longing with
positive action.

← wise owl

Mr. Alexander's
Four Steps to Love
will make you feel hotter
than a fur-lined
go-go boot!

← stiletto

I see more happiness, more cuteness,

and perhaps an exciting

new skill in your future.

Lucky number: 18

↑
fortune
cookie

STEP 1

MAKING THE LIST

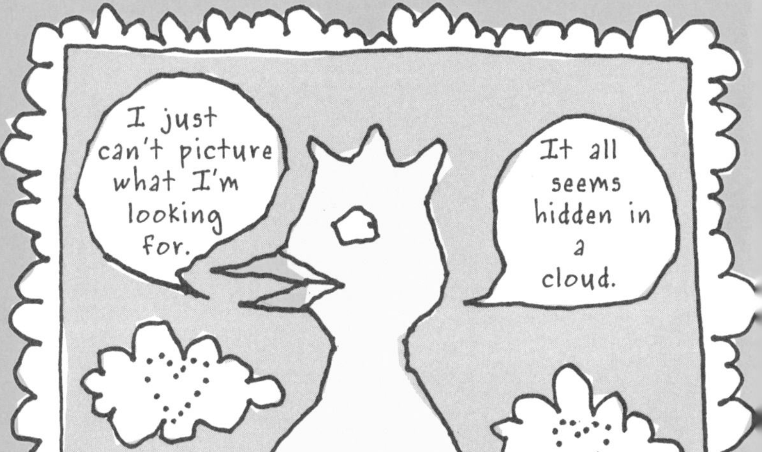

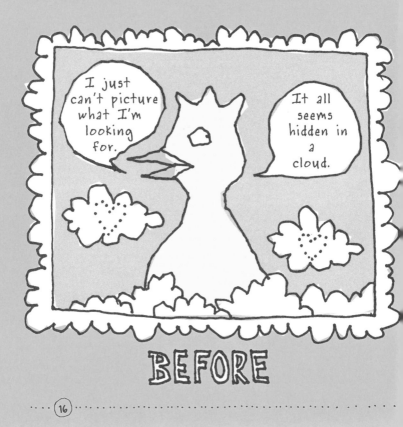

BEFORE

AFTER

Wow! Now I have a vision of what I'm looking for. Making this list has helped me create an image of my dream partner in my mind. I'm going to send that vision out into the world and see what happens.

In Step 1:
• List all the qualities you want in your perfect partner

• Think about which qualities are most meaningful to you

• Send your wish list out into the world

• Bake wish list cookies for extra credit

Step 1: The Nuts and Bolts

n Step 1, you will write a list of every quality
ou're looking for in an ideal partner. Once you've
ade your wish list, you are going to send it out
nto the world in a way that seems appropriate to you.

he reason for making this list is twofold. First,
nd most importantly, it changes your outlook on
hat is possible. You learn to ask not for something
cceptable, but for something wonderful. Making a
st impels you to think about the world as a
enerous place rather than a stingy one.

he second thing it does is to force you to think
bout what you really want and replace abstract
onging for happiness with a concrete way of
hinking about what makes you happy. You'll
iscover that there are certain things that are highly
mportant to you and other things that may have
eemed really important but are not essential.

Create Your Dream Partner... on Paper

For this first step you will need paper and pen. Start writing down everything that you would want in your dream partner. Don't worry about things being too weird or selfish or silly or unrealistic to put on your list. Just write them down.

You may not complete your list in one sitting. Once you've started, other qualities might occur to you. You can keep a notebook and jot things down as they pop into your head. If you work better with another person, find a good friend who knows you and your dating history. She can remind you of that guy you broke up with because he didn't close the bathroom door.

Ask for Everything!

Asking for the moon gives you a much better chance of actually reaching it. Sometimes we think our luck will disappear if we ask for more, that if things are going okay, we should stay small and quiet so we won't be disappointed or thought of as greedy. Think, instead, that the world's generosity knows no limits.

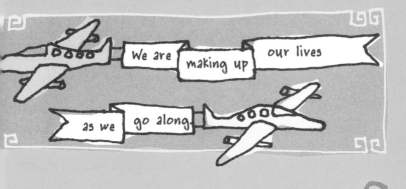

We are making up our lives as we go along.

"I can't believe that whatever force it is that keeps the spheres revolving in the heavens is going to stop to give me a red bicycle. . . . [But] if prayer were a way in which you aligned your body with the forces that flow through the universe, then I would accept prayer."
—Quentin Crisp

You improve your chances by making your wishes more tangible. When you put them out there where you can see them, it becomes easier to act on them. But it also means that you have to be brave enough to get your hopes up. Dream a big dream. If you can imagine it, you are one step closer to finding it.

Asking for everything alters your situation in a funny way. It makes you think about who you'd be if you were someone who **always** asked for everything. It also puts a kind of excited, positive, and happy vibration out into the world. Is it possible that you actually **could** have someone who makes you deliriously happy? What would happen if you started to believe that was true?

When people begin to make a list, they usually put down about ten dream partner qualities and then throw down the pen in despair. "This is impossible," they say. "There's nobody out there that's this perfect!" But whether your dream partner exists or not is immaterial just now. **The point of making the list is to explore what happens when you ask for everything** So . . .

Ask Ask Ask Ask Ask Ask Ask Ask Ask
Ask Ask Ask Ask Ask Ask Ask Ask Ask Ask
Ask Ask Ask Ask Ask Ask Ask Ask Ask Ask
Ask Ask Ask Ask Ask Ask Ask Ask Ask

What kinds of things go on a list?

You can list physical qualities (body type, hair color), descriptions of temperament (excitable, mellow), things they will do for you as well as things they won't, money matters, interests, biases you'll share, qualities they'll bring out in you, ways they'll make you feel, issues involving the realm of ooh la la, things they'll appreciate about you, political convictions, feelings about family, things they'll cut you slack for.

Here are a few more ideas, in case you need inspiration.

What Will My Dream Lover Do?

Bring me chocolates...breakfast in bed...toasted
cheese sandwiches and tomato soup when I'm blue ♡
Tell stupid jokes ♡ Make the bed ♡ Clean the bathroom
♡ Be charmed by my family's eccentricities ♡
Run her own business ♡ Think I'm smart...
beautiful...funny...singular...the best ♡
Have a good sense of direction ♡ Like to go camping
♡ Dance well ♡ Be a champ in the sack ♡
Speak eloquently ♡ Know about many things ♡
Like to throw parties ♡ Weave ♡ Be good at puzzles
♡ Cry easily ♡ Never cry ♡ Run fast ♡ Walk slowly
♡ Speak softly ♡ Speak low ♡ Wear heels
♡ Collect stamps ♡ Love dogs ♡ Have a past ♡
Know how to navigate by the stars ♡ Sing ♡
Storm the tower ♡ Like walks in the rain
♡ Be able to sit still ♡ Give lots of money to charity ♡
Be coordinated ♡ Know all the words to "Half Breed"
♡ Pay bills on time ♡ Swim with sharks ♡ Fear nothing
♡ Write me a note every morning ♡ Rub my neck
♡ Cut my hair ♡ Have sweet breath

What Will My Dream Lover Be Like?

Funny ♡ Hard working ♡ Lazy ♡ Sentimental
♡ Morally upstanding ♡ Louche and hedonistic ♡
Proper ♡ Gauche ♡ Quiet ♡ Boisterous ♡ Silent ♡
Mysterious ♡ Delicate ♡ Brilliant ♡ A sexual dynamo
Wry ♡ Befuddled ♡ Goofy ♡ Cool ♡ Debonair ♡ Gawky
♡ Moody ♡ Merry ♡ Adventurous ♡ A homebody

Is there a spot where you feel especially good?
Go there to make your wish list.

I go to the lingerie section at Neiman's!

I light a fragrant vanilla candle in my coop.

When I am making wishes, I like to rest
in the cool darkness of my cookie jar.
Lucky number: 28.

What Will My Dream Lover Look Like?

Smoldering with a broken nose ♡ Pale and wan ♡
Elegant with long limbs ♡ Sexy with a belly like
Madonna's in 1984 ♡ Dark and sophisticated ♡ Tall
♡ Small ♡ Fit as a fiddle ♡ Curvy and luscious ♡
Curly hair ♡ Thick eyebrows ♡ Beautiful feet ♡
Rosy cheeks ♡ Eyes as black as midnight ♡
Heart-shaped lips ♡ Dimples ♡ Broad shoulders
♡ Unpolished ♡ Exotic ♡ Plain ♡ Wild hair ♡ No hair ♡
Some hair some of the time ♡ Big butt ♡
Small butt ♡ Perfectly formed ears ♡
Skin like honey...cream...chocolate ♡ Nice teeth
♡ Beautiful oval knees

Has curly red hair
☆ Needs to read more than
the backs of cereal boxes
Gets along with my cat

What Are Your Non-Negotiables?

As your list takes shape, you'll find that there are certain qualities that speak to you. Maybe they make your toes curl. You might shiver even though it's not cold. These qualities are your "non-negotiables."

Mark these qualities with a star. At the same time that you're putting all your wishes out there and asking for the moon, you are focusing on what you'd really **like** to have versus the things you think you **have** to have in a partner.

☆Wants to have a family

Is taller than I am

Has his own money

Wears glasses

Drives fast

☆Likes to eat

Wanda's List

Here's a sample list from Wanda, a 28-year-old real estate photographer.

1. Has brown eyes

2. Likes to two-step

3. Looks out for his grandma

4. Makes me laugh

☆ 5. Loves to go to the movies

6. Brings me things (flowers, etc.)

7. Can speak more than one language (Chinese?)

8. Doesn't suck up to my mother

9. Thinks my mole is beautiful

0. Has nice long legs

1. Enjoys Patti Smith

2. Makes sweet love to me all the time

3. Likes his work

4. Will buy me presents

5. Thinks that I am the best person on Earth

6. Does not pick his nose in front of me

7. Likes to make out on the couch

8. Is not nervous around birds

9. Has just a little bit of rhythm

0. Can cook a meal in under 45 minutes

Ned's List

This list comes from Ned, a 44-year-old fun-loving elementary school teacher.

1. Must have well-clipped toenails

2. Has a sense of humor

3. Has been through some hard times but got back on his feet and gained some wisdom

4. Handsome

5. Dark hair (not necessarily on his head)

6. Hairy

7. Supports self with a reasonable income

☆ 8. Patient

9. Flexible

0. Can afford to travel and eat out

1. Acts on generous impulses

2. Pulls over to help someone stranded on the side of the road

3. Strong arms

4. Doesn't snore

5. Likes to sing (but is not a trained singer)

6. Plays acoustic guitar

7. Is social (gets along with people)

8. Is healthy (but not obsessive about it)

9. Likes to travel

0. Really likes flea markets a lot

1. Takes the road not taken

2. Has memorized some poetry (Robert Frost or epic poems)

☆ 23. Likes recreational camping (with flannel sleeping bags and my pancakes)

24. Has a warm family (real people, not necessarily a perfect family)

25. Appreciates the beauty in ordinary objects

26. Would be okay with me getting in a dark mood for a couple of days

27. Would expect the best from me

28. Would bring out the best in me

29. Would value that I expect the best from him

30. Has learned a lot about letting go

31. Is really in touch with his body and is not ashamed of one little imperfection and likes to be tangled up in a big snake knot

32. Thinks I'm cute

33. Has a crush on me

4. Likes my stuff (radio collection, camera collection, my religious icons)

5. Clicks with me sexually

6. Likes to curl up on the couch

7. Likes channel surfing

8. Likes foreign movies but is not above going to see a blockbuster

9. Definitely not a snob

0. Not judgmental of me (but would gang up with me on someone else—all in fun, of course)

1. Knows that there are times when I need to be comforted

Extra Credit

Wish List Cookies

Wish list cookies are not only delicious, they also make a pretty good spell.

Makes approximately 50 cookies

1/2 cup (118 ml) unsalted butter (for sensuality)

2 medium eggs (for change)

3/4 cup (170 g) sugar (for sweetness)

1 tsp. (5 ml) vanilla (for romance)

2 cups (220 g) flour (for strength)

1/2 tsp. (.5 g) baking powder (for spark)

1/4 tsp. (.25 g) salt (for intelligence)

1/2 cup (115 g) crushed sugar cubes (for something ext

1. Cream butter, eggs, sugar, and vanilla. In a separate bowl, sift flour, baking powder, and salt. Add dry to wet and mix well.

2. Wrap dough tightly in plastic wrap and chill in freezer for 45 minutes.

3. Preheat oven to 350°F (175° C).

4. Roll out dough to 1/8th inch (1/3 cm) thick.

5. Take a cookie cutter in the shape of a little man or a little woman or a heart and cut the cookie dough. As you create each cookie, earmark it with a quality or trait from your list. Cut out a cookie and think to yourself, "Likes Dolly Parton." Cut out a cookie and think, "Is an Eagles fan." As you cut out each cookie, concentrate on each new wish.

6. Sprinkle each cookie with crushed sugar cubes like Tinkerbell's magic dust.

7. Take all of your wishes and bake for 8–10 minutes until golden brown.

8. After the cookies cool, you can go further and write your wishes on the cookies with frosting.

9. Enjoy or give away.

Put It Out There!

Once your list feels complete, it's time to send it out into the unknown. Remember the note from Jane and Michael Banks in **Mary Poppins**? The two children write a want ad describing a perfect nanny. Although the ad gets shredded by their father and thrown into the fireplace, it floats up the chimney and out into the night sky. The next day, Mary Poppins arrives.

By making their list, Jane and Michael conjured up their perfect nanny. By making your list, you are announcing your wishes to yourself and to the powers that be. You are declaring your belief that they can come true. By physically putting your wish list out into the world, you are making it more concrete and real.

Making your wishes known (even just to yourself) makes it easier for them to be fulfilled.

Make a copy of the list, seal it in an envelope, and put it in a drawer for safekeeping.

Now launch the original list into the cosmos in any of the following ways:

Burn the list.

Place it on train tracks and watch as an oncoming train flattens it.

Bury it beneath your favorite magnolia tree.

Throw a small party and read it aloud before tearing it up.

Attach it to a string and fly it in the air like a kite.

Use the classic "message in a bottle" method.

Get your list—and your wishes—out there!

Your Mental Most-Wanted Poster

The process of making this list has given you a kind of "most-wanted poster" to refer to when you are out and about in the world, meeting new people. Now that you have the words "must have a nice baritone" or "cowboy boots" cued in your head, you're more attuned to the signals that are sure to crop up around you. Perhaps you'll be out buying cheese at the grocery store when you hear someone with a melodious voice in back of you talking about a perfect pair of cowboy boots. Having drafted your list, you'll be more likely to turn around and give that person the eye.

> After making my list, I insulated my coop with all 43 pages of it!

> A creative and practical solution. Well done! Now that you know who you are looking for, are you ready to come out of your shell in Step 2?

> Indeed I am!

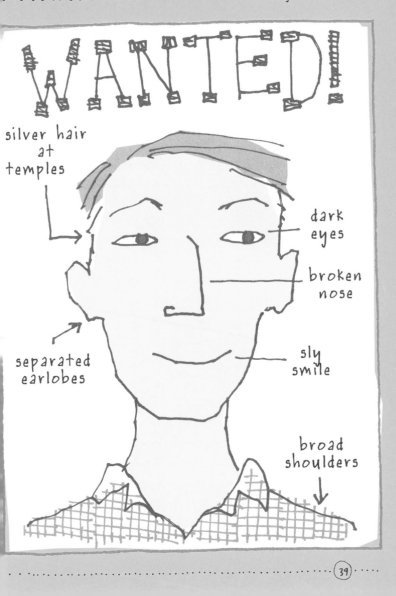

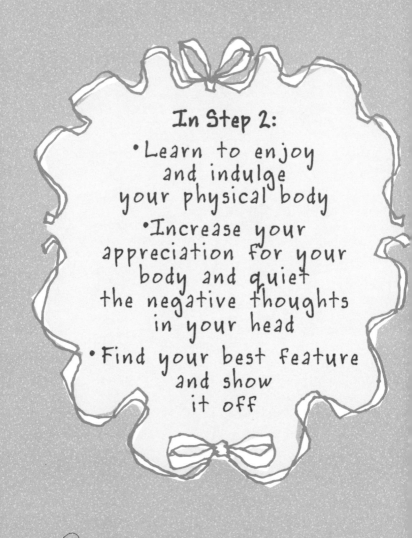

In Step 2:

- Learn to enjoy
  and indulge
  your physical body

- Increase your
  appreciation for your
  body and quiet
  the negative thoughts
  in your head

- Find your best feature
  and show
  it off

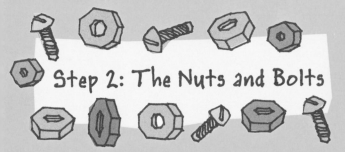

Step 2: The Nuts and Bolts

n Step 1, you were thinking, thinking, thinking. It
as all about your head. Now, in Step 2, you are
oing to move on to your body. First, you will
earn to treat your body better as a way of
nspiring it to start releasing more mojo juice.*
hen you will learn to delight in the things about
ou that are beautiful.

reating your body better—in the way you think
bout it and the things you do to and for it—will
ncourage it to go to work for you.

tep 2 also involves making yourself feel more
ppealing. You will figure out what your best
eature is and then perform one small action to
lorify that feature and feel more magnetic. Feeling
ttractive increases the power of your love magnet.

Your love essence, the unquantifiable thing that draws others
o you.

Moving Back into Your Body

We spend a lot of time in our heads, but the fact is, we are made up of both a mind **and** a body. We can often forget that we are sensual beings made of flesh and blood. This chapter is not about perfecting the way your body **looks**; it's about habits that will improve the way your body **feels** and the way you feel about your body.

Living in your body can be harder than it should be. Most people are hypercritical of themselves and the way they look. Step 2 offers a recipe for trading in those put-downs for praise by glorying in the parts of you that are most fetching.

Good Habits to Cultivate

Smiling: Everywhere, all the time. When you don't think you have anything to smile about, just think about what's good in your life (your house, family, new shoes, job, tasty sandwich, that five extra dollars in your pocket...).

Deep and steady breathing: When you leave the house each day; when you put the coffee pot on; when you happen by a flowering bush or plant; when you are exercising; when you're upset or nervous; when you lay down to sleep.

Pulling your shoulders back: While sitting at a desk or table; when walking up stairs; when you feel stressed or blue or small.

Holding your head up: When you are outside so you can look at cloud formations. Look at the sky instead of the sidewalk.

Standing or sitting up straight: At dinner; at your desk; when waiting on line at the multiplex; when checking out people and their pets in the park.

Looking people in the eye: As much as possible. People respond when you acknowledge them.

Tending to Your Body

When people or things are neglected, they wither and droop. But when you nourish and pay attention to people, plants, dogs, chickens, etc., they bloom and perk up.

Try treating your physical self with this type of nourishing attention.

Take baths ♡ Put soft sheets on your bed ♡
♡ Stretch ♡ Nap ♡ Dress up ♡
♡ Put on underwear that makes you feel sexy, beautiful, or comfortable ♡
♡ Rub cream into your skin ♡ Get a massage
♡ Float in a pool, lake, or swimming hole
♡ Dance around your living room

Tending to your physical self will help you climb back into your body. Spoiling your body is a way of inspiring it to go out into the world and begin aiding and abetting you in your search for love.

What Is Cute?

Often it seems that we measure how attractive we are by how well we "fit in" or match a standard. We work to downplay the parts of ourselves that don't fit a mold. That effort is much better spent highlighting the features that **do** work for us.

Consider the women you find enchanting and the men you find magnetic. What is it about them? Are they perfect? Probably not. Chances are, you don't need other people to be perfect to find them appealing. See what happens when you apply that same level of acceptance to yourself.

Over the course of one day, keep a running tab of how many times you fret over something about yourself that you don't like. Keep a small pad in your pocket and make a check mark every time you criticize your body. Let's say that you counted 24 moments of cursing your love handles. The following day, try to tell yourself 24 times how beautiful your mouth is.

OK   NICE   CUTE   VERY   SUPER   HOT   WICKED
                          CUTE   CUTE   HOT

Entertain a more expansive idea of beauty, an idea of beauty that **includes** rather than rejects. Ease up on the pressure to conform to an ideal. As we learned on page 43, this works in two ways: Going through life liking your body is much more pleasant than the alternative; it also creates a natural guy/chick magnet.

Today is a new day.
Shake off those silly ideas
about what is pretty and what isn't.
You're beautiful, damn it!

The Bald and the Beautiful

Here's an example of how your attitude affects your cuteness, as told to me by a charming man who learned how to strut his stuff.

Testify!

"For as long as I could remember, when I looked in a mirror, all I saw was a Buddha belly and a bald head. I beat myself up over these features endlessly. I would say to myself, 'You are **bald** and you are **fat**.' When I felt bad, my reflection looked balder and fatter.

"One day, I saw a man walking down the street. He was about 55 years old and had a big belly and a shiny, bald head. It was a sunny day and he was smiling and strutting like a rooster.

Mmm, rooster.

"His expression and his bearing suggested that he expected everyone—men, women, and dogs—to follow him to the ends of the earth. I had to agree. He carried himself like a million bucks.

In that instant, I realized that neither his **fatness** nor his **baldness** was a barrier to **cuteness**; it all had to do with how he saw himself.

Strangely, since I've eased up on myself, more and more people want to date me. I haven't grown any less bald or any less fat, I just like myself better and people seem to be responding to it. Whenever I hear the bald-hating voice in my head, I repeat my mantra: **Think of the strutter, think of the strutter!"**

Take the physical characteristics that you don't like and lighten up on them. When that negative thought creeps into your head about your Sasquatch feet/skinny little bird legs/flat ass/tiny boobs/bony arms/saggy belly/dry, unmanageable hair/bumpy skin/thick ankles/stubby fingers/malformed ears/lazy eye, put it on the back burner. In its place, put a thought about your long eyelashes/strong hands/soulful eyes/shapely forearms/generous mouth/juicy earlobes/gorgeous gams/curving neck/bountiful booty. (See page 54 for tips on how to make yourself a visual reminder.)

Feeling cuter draws people to you like moths to a flame.

What's Your Best Thing?

If you are going to be focusing on something good, you need to know what that thing is. Let's figure out what your best feature is and find a way to show it off.

> I used to want to be one of those plain, tasteful ballet flats, but now I know that my curvy instep is my best feature! I'm so happy to be an embroidered faux snakeskin stiletto!

> For years, I longed to be a cream-filled sandwich cookie, but now I embrace my subtle almond flavor and architectural form.
> Lucky Number: 88.

The Special Feature Teacher

You can figure out your best feature in several ways. Even if you already think you know what it is, you may discover that you have three or four more. Stand in front of a mirror. Wear as much or as little as you want. Put on the clothes that make you feel your best. (If self-esteem is not quite up to snuff, see "A Letter to Your Brain" in "The Toolkit," page 93.) Look at your body one feature at a time. Change the lighting if you wish. Spend a few minutes gazing at yourself from different angles. What part of your body makes you look twice or grin or pat it with satisfaction? What is the most beautiful part of you?

Look at your body the way someone who is madly in love with you would.

Δ·Δ·Δ·Δ·Δ·Δ·Δ·Δ·

You can also look for clues in your all-time favorite picture of yourself. What do you like about it? Your smile? Your right bicep?

Look in your closet. What's your favorite garment or accessory: a scarf, perfectly worn jeans, a piece of jewelry? What do you always reach for? Why? Is it the color? The way it fits? Does it accentuate some part of you? Figuring out why you gravitate toward certain parts of your wardrobe will make it easier for you to figure out what's best about your body.

Remember the subtle, sometimes ignored, features — the nape of the neck, hands, fingers, ears, knees, calves, and ankles. Any part of you, no matter how small or large, can be magnificent.

> I asked all my friends what my best feature was, and everybody said it was my eyes. So I had my friend Fernanda come over and show me how to put on eye makeup. While she was at it, she taught me about lipstick. Now I have two best features!

Make a Visual Reminder

Fill in the blanks on the certificate below and repeat the simple statements to yourself whenever you need a gentle reminder to stop harping on a much-maligned body part. You can copy the text onto a card and carry it in your wallet or tape it to a mirror so it's always handy and visible.

My _____ is/are so beautiful.
So is/are my _____.
I love the way it/they _____,
_____, and _____.
I always beat myself up about my _____.
I'm sorry, _____; I will try to
be nicer to you in the future. After all,
you are the only _____ that I've got.
And without you, I couldn't _____.

Mirror, mirror on the wall,
what feature of mine . . .
could cause a brawl?
Is a legend of the fall?
Is ready to have a ball?
Brings traffic to a crawl?
Is neither overly large
or much too small?
Is the fairest of them all?

Haiku for You

Honor your feature in poetry. Write an ode, poem, song, or haiku praising your best feature.

> intoxicating
> smooth as silk and oft hidden
> elegant elbow

> so much like sea shells
> a deeper pink when I'm mad
> my ears speak volumes

> round as two beach balls
> both defying gravity
> perfect buns of steel

> silently speaking
> untamed yet so civilized
> expressive eyebrows

The Mysterious Scarves
of French Women

What is it about French women? They always look so good. At first I thought that it had to do with scarves: French women must be trained in grade school in the ways of the artfully tied scarf. Also, their scarves never fall off. The squares of cloth seem to float above their shoulders, cloaking them in elegance, never moving unless they want them to. I can barely make my muffler stay on!

French women are doing something mysterious and almost Zen-like with their scarves.

For a long time I believed this scarf theory, until one day I saw a scarfless mademoiselle buying aspirin in a pharmacy.

She was about 19 years old, and she was lovely. She was beautifully curvy with creamy skin and very dark, velvety eyes. Her hair was tied in a bun. Her sweater was cut in a deep V to show off her **belle poitrine**. She was also about 30 pounds over her fighting weight, and she had no chin to speak of.

It didn't matter. She walked in beauty like the night. That's when it came to me. She was not wearing a scarf, but she had that quality that I had perceived before.

The beauty of French women has nothing to do with scarves. It has to do with their ability to discern what about them is extraordinary and make the most of it.

I thought to myself, "This young woman, if she lived back home, would be wearing a track suit and hoping that no one would look at her." And there she was in the pain-reliever aisle, delighting me with her loveliness, beholden to no one, beautiful enough for the eyes of all the world.

Accentuating Your Positives

Hanging my head out the window of a high tower helps people to notice my long hair.

 • Eyes: Try on naughty librarian eyeglasses. Frame your eyes with your hands frequently, as if you are directing a scene in a movie

• Ears: Tuck your hair behind your ear languorously. Cultivate sideburns.

• Nose: Give yourself long
bangs or a middle part.
Run your index finger along
the bridge of your nose.

• Mouth: Pop a lollipop
into your mouth.
Yawn frequently. Pout.

• Neck/chest: Lightly dust on
shimmery powder. Cup
boobs lovingly. Wear thick
gold chains or tight shirts.

Hands: Put on a big ring
you can play with.
Gesture animatedly.
Get a prop, like a magic
wand, to carry around.

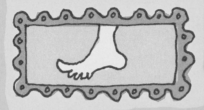

• Feet: Wear sandals, go barefoot, or wear a jangly anklet. Step on someone's toes while dancing.

• Waist: Grab a hula hoop. Strap on a leather belt with a big buckle.

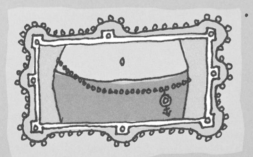

• Hips: Sashay up and down or stick your thumbs into the front pockets of your jeans and lean against a wall. Think James Dean.

Legs: Zip up calf- or knee-length boots (depending on which part of your leg is most shapely), or just pull on some crazy leg warmers. Wear shorts. Draw the eye to your rugby thighs by applying calamine lotion to an imaginary bug bite.

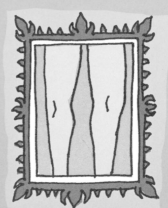

· Back: Get a temporary tattoo. Offer someone a piggyback ride. Chop wood in a tank top.

Tush: Smack your bottom to emphasize a point. Walk into a room backward.

Jenelle's Tale

Remember that you are doing Step 2 for yourself, not just to attract others to you. We are perhaps most attractive when we are happy with ourselves and not trying to lure someone. Take, for example, the story of my friend Jenelle:

Once, when I was in college, Jenelle showed up at our metalsmithing class looking like the love child of a rock star and an angel. She was wearing a purple lace bra, cut-off shorts, and hiking boots. He hair was piled up on top of her head and her little belly was gleaming in the sun. There she was, welding away, beauty and strength fused into one glorious being.

I figured that she had a crush on one of the guys in the class, and that she had dressed especially for him. I asked her if that was the case.

"No," she said.

"Are you in love?" I asked.

"No," she answered. "Why do you ask?"

"Well, you look so good . . . I was just wondering why you were dressed that way."

"It's not for anyone, really," said Jenelle, smiling.

"I'm just trying to add to the erotic energy of
the universe."

There are other reasons to be beautiful than to
please other people. We can be beautiful for our
own pleasure or, like Jenelle said, to make the world
sexier, prettier, and more fun.

When you are going out (or even staying in), think
about how you can add to the erotic energy of the
universe in your own special way.

Ready for the Road Test?

Do you take this body, to have
and to hold, from this day forward?

lthough you can of course keep amending the list
rom Step 1, that step has a distinct beginning,
niddle, and end. But Step 2 is different. Ideally, you
ever really complete Step 2. Choices about the way
ou think about your body and the way you want
o treat it will come up several times a day. At each
noment you'll use the new habits that you've created
nd your best feature as signposts that steer you
oward a more rewarding connection with your body.

Step 2 has
made me feel so
good! I'm radiant,
magnificent,
exquisite, divine!
I want to share
all my goodness
with the
world!

Then it's time to get out there
and say, "Hello, world!"
Step 3 will show you how!

STEP 3
JOINING UP

"Hey, Chicken, do you want to come to a party?"
Who knew all these people would drop out of the sky?
"Hey, Chicken, have you met my brother?"
"Hey, Chicken, will you escort me to a fancy museum benefit?"

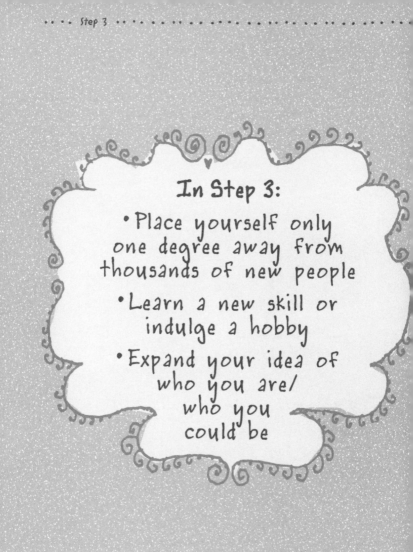

In Step 3:

- Place yourself only one degree away from thousands of new people

- Learn a new skill or indulge a hobby

- Expand your idea of who you are/ who you could be

Step 3: The Nuts and Bolts

> You are one step away from meeting 2,000 new people.

At a certain point, I noticed that I was going on more dates than most of my friends. I tried to investigate why that was. I came to the conclusion that it had to do with being out in the world. I was talking to people, taking classes, working in a restaurant, and volunteering. I was interacting with people all day long. The reason I was getting more dates than my friends was because more people had the opportunity to meet me.

Now that you've finished Step 2, you're going to take your show on the road. In Step 3, you are going to pick up a skill, learn something new, **and** meet new people.

It's all based on simple math. Most people—even shy ones—know at least 200 people if you count family, coworkers, childhood friends, college drinking buddies, neighbors, doctors, dentists, bus drivers, dog trainers, and hash slingers. If you join a class, club, team, or other group that is composed of at least ten people you don't already know, you are expanding your circle of love exponentially. You are now within reach of 2,000 new people!

This Just In: Wine-Tasting Class Debunks "Over-30" Myth

> There's nobody out there.

> All the good ones are married.

> Ugh.

Wanda's friends kept telling her that once you were 30 years old, there were no more eligible men. She found that depressing. Worst of all, it seemed true. When she got to Step 3, she decided to take a wine-tasting class. She liked wine but had never really been interested in wine-tasting. She took the class because she was interested in meeting an affluent man who liked to go out to dinner. She figured that a man like that would take a wine-tasting class.

The first night, she was amazed. There were 15 men in the room over the age of 30, and half of them were single. She realized that what her friends had been telling her was a myth. Then one of the guys in the class said he had a handsome cousin named Fernando . . .

Where Do You Sign Up?

How, you may ask, do you join up? Asking yourself a few questions can open your mind to the many possibilities and narrow your choices down to your most interesting options. The suggestions that follow might stir a memory or long-buried ambition. Keep notes as you read through the next few pages and then look to them for direction.

FUNFUNFUNFUNFUN

What Do You Enjoy Doing?

Reading ♡ Writing ♡ Swimming in a creek
♡ Strolling through a grove of trees ♡
Watching Jane Austen movies ♡ Staying in
Going out ♡ Playing with your cat ♡
♡ Dancing like a maniac, maniac on the floor ♡
Drinking Belgian beer ♡ Going to the opera
♡ Going to minor league baseball games ♡
Playing games ♡ Scrabble, anyone?
♡ Going on road trips ♡ Running ♡ Bicycling ♡
Snapping black-and-white photos of strangers
♡ Barbecuing ribs ♡ Volunteering with kids ♡
Gymnastics

FUNFUNFUNFUNFUN

FUNFUNFUNFUNFUN

What Have You Always Wanted to Learn?

Bungee jumping ♡ Scuba diving ♡ Belly dancing ♡
Stand-up comedy ♡ How to cry on cue ♡ Stripping
♡ Taxidermy ♡ How to prepare coq au vin ♡
Wine appreciation ♡ Sewing ♡ Upholstering ♡ Rowing
♡ The French horn ♡ Cake decorating ♡
How to change your oil ♡ Mountain climbing ♡
Container gardening ♡ How to draw comic strips
♡ Yoga ♡ The tango

FUNFUNFUNFUN

Branch Out

In Step 3 you have a chance to take a vacation from your normal self and everyday life, so try to branch out. If you are a chef, steer clear of a cooking class. If you are a psychiatrist, shy away from conferences on post-traumatic stress disorder.

While these activities can add to your professional acumen and skill level, it is wiser and more fun to expand your horizons. You get extra credit for doing something you never thought you would do.

You can try on different things until you find a good fit. This step is more about the **experience** and less about the **result**. For example, it can be liberating to be the worst in the class and not care. Take a class just to explore what it's like to be **bad** at something!

Wrestling with Fate

I was always the boy who was picked last for teams. I was convinced I was bad at sports into my early adulthood. One day, a person noticed my sturdy body and low center of gravity and blithely asked if I was a wrestler. I stepped outside of myself and pondered the question. "Hmm," I thought. "I've never tried to wrestle. Maybe, just maybe, I am a wrestler." So I joined up for a wrestling team, and guess what? I AM good at it. It takes a Mack Truck to knock me down!

Step 3 is a chance to discover all the people you **could** be that you may have decided that, for no good reason, you couldn't possibly be. Maybe you're not shy but like to listen as much as gab. Maybe you're a delightful dancer despite a bad prom experience. Maybe you're a good cook who never experiments because it's too much hassle. Stepping into an untried activity will help you reshape the way you see yourself.

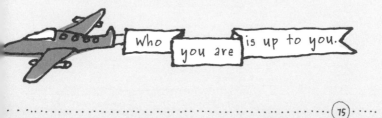

Who you are is up to you.

How Do You Find Out About Stuff?

Yellow pages. Community centers. Learning Annex booklets. Continuing education classes at local colleges. Independent and local newspapers. Bulletin boards at coffee shops. Friends. The person in the next cubicle. Alumni associations. Chalk messages on the sidewalk. Health club fliers. Your mail.

Use the Internet

Typing "Akron tap dancing adult" into a search engine will lead you to a list of Akron Community Centers, as well as the five branches of the Akron Area YMCA.

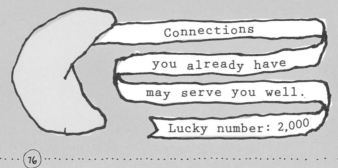

Connections

you already have

may serve you well.

Lucky number: 2,000

Where Do People Gather?

Bookstores have book clubs, signings, and lectures.

Museums, theaters, and orchestras have educational and recreational programs.

Galleries have opening-night parties for exhibits.

High-school booster clubs have fund-raisers.

Craft shops host workshops, knitting circles, and quilting bees.

Wine shops have wine tastings.

Country-western bars have line dancing.

Health clubs have regular mixers.

Nonprofits, from the Humane Society to Habitat for Humanity, have volunteer opportunities.

Bars and pubs have weekly quiz nights.

And darts!

Start a Group

If you can't find what you want, consider creating your own group.

To recruit new blood, put up posters or fliers in your favorite hangouts. Ask your friends to spread the word. Post a message in your favorite chat room.

Ballroom dancing was too obvious, so I'm starting a clogging club!

Although it ruffled a few feathers, I started a fan club for Gregory Peck!

My juggling group meets monthly in my VW bug.

If I start a book club, I can meet bookworms.

I see an astrology club in my future. Lucky number: 234.

Improving Your Odds

You've now improved those odds we were talking about in the introduction. By putting yourself in the path of 2,000 new people, you have greatly improved your chances of meeting somebody good. If you chose to do something you had never done before, you may have discovered that there were aspects of you that have been hidden or denied or forgotten. Who knows who you are going to meet? Who knows who you are going to become?

In Step 3, you exercised the "new experience" portion of your brain.

I'm coming out of my shell! I feel like love is just a few pages away.

Stop searching forever. Happiness is right next to you. Lucky number: 1.

STEP 4
BECOMING YOUR BEST PARTNER

BEFORE
Mr. Alexander's Four Steps to Love

AFTER
Mr. Alexander's Four Steps to Love

In Step 4:

• Pick three things from your Step 1 list and take them on for yourself

• Gain the tools to cultivate these qualities on an ongoing basis

• Become your own dream partner

Step 4: The Nuts and Bolts

Let's think about where you've been and where you're going.

Step 1 gave you a clearer idea of what and who you're looking for. Step 2 helped you feel cuter, so now you're giving off a juicy new vibe. And in Step 3, you took that clarity and that cuteness for a spin. In Step 4, you are going to stop looking outside yourself for satisfaction. Rather than focusing on finding someone else to bring love into your life, Step 4 is going to push you to love **yourself** more.

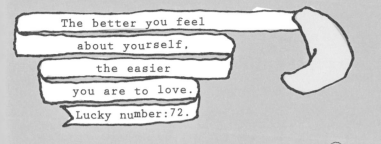

The better you feel
about yourself,
the easier
you are to love.
Lucky number: 72.

Step 4 encourages you to stop waiting—to be happy, to not feel lonely, to feel strong, to feel complete. Instead of waiting, you're going to take some of the qualities that were really important to you from your list and try to develop them in yourself.

It's time to take your original list out of the drawer and look it over. Think about the qualities you starred. Why did you star them? Is there anything you'd now like to add to or subtract from your list? As you are considering your list, choose three qualities that speak to you, whether they were originally starred or not. You're going to be working on developing or deepening these qualities in yourself, so keep that in mind as you make your choices. You could choose one that's very important to you, one that's sort of important, and one that just seems fun. Your choices will give you one that might be difficult to work on, one that will be easy, and one that will be just right.

ample Sets of Three

Likes to travel

Has a warm family

Strong arms

Can dance

Has a global vision

Accepts my shoe problem

Wicked sense of humor

Likes cats

In good shape

When I was 10 years old, my grandmother told me that Lana Turner was discovered by a Hollywood talent scout while having an ice cream sundae at Schwab's. That story to me was more exciting than any fairy tale.

But one day I realized that I had spent my whole life waiting for the talent scout to find me. Professionally, I'd thought I didn't really have to make or do anything for people to recognize that I was talented. I **knew** that someone with a lot of power and money was going to talk to me one day on the street, see how clever I was, and give me a great job.

I believed this about my emotional life as well. I **knew** there was somebody out there who was going to come along and take care of all of my craziness/neuroses/loose ends and make me happy.

But time passed, and I noticed that although I was waiting very patiently, it had been a long time and no one had shown up. No one had given me that great job, and no one I had dated had miraculously transformed my world.

I decided to stop waiting. I thought, "I know what qualities I've been looking for in a partner, but the partner with those qualities isn't here yet. If I want those things in my life, I'm going to have to find them in myself."

I'm going to fix it myself!

How Do You Develop a Quality, Exactly?

Quality—Likes to travel: Go on a trip, be it a day trip to the country or a grand tour of China. Take a bus downtown.

Quality—Has a warm family: Try to resolve a problem you have with a family member, plan a small reunion, make a weekly phone call to your sister.

Quality—Strong arms: Do pull-ups. Do push-ups. Take yoga. Practice archery. Row, row, row your boat.

Quality—Accepts my shoe problem: Celebrate your shoes! Buy special plastic boxes in which to store them. Polish them. Shine them. Buff them. Enshrine them. Loan a favorite pair to someone and see how it makes you feel.

Quality—Likes cats: Volunteer at an animal refuge. Go to the zoo and study the lions. Enrich your relationship with your own cat.

It's not that you have stopped looking for these qualities in someone else or that the qualities that you didn't choose to take on are unimportant. You are still seeking someone with strong arms and a warm family who understands your shoe problem. But now you are looking for those qualities because you find them attractive, not because you need them to make yourself feel complete.

The Effects of Step 4

Wanda wrote "will buy me presents" on her list and marked it with a star (see page 29). Because it seemed doable, she decided the first thing she would take on would be buying herself a present once a week.

It wasn't easy. She found herself rationalizing the purchases she had made. Things had been on sale, she really needed a new pair of shoes, the books she bought would help her career. A quality that had seemed easy to take on proved complicated, and trying to take it on forced Wanda to confront how stingy she was with herself. Once she identified this stinginess, she began to notice it in other aspects of her life. She had a hard time letting herself relax and do nothing, even if it was just for 5 minutes. Buying a present—even if it was a bottle of nice shampoo—was a way to be kinder to herself and a reminder to treat herself nicely.

Taking on some of the qualities will be fun, taking on some of the qualities will be difficult—but all of them will take you somewhere.

Post Notes to Self

Take your three qualities and copy each one onto six sticky notes. Place them in key areas around your house, in your car, at work, on your bathroom mirror, inside the cookie jar, and any other place where you spend a lot of time.

Being more fulfilled also makes you cuter! The bald man in Step 2 was attractive because he liked himself. The man who plays Tony Soprano is an extra-hot dreamboat because of something inside him. Jenelle was beautiful for herself and therefore irresistible to everyone else. And under those scarves, those French women know they look good—damn good. So while Step 4 is designed to make you happier, don't dismiss its ability to make you more appealing, too!

The Toolkit

As an added bonus for completing **Mr. Alexander's Four Steps to Love**, you also get this handy toolkit, free with purchase. Here are some tools to use while you are doing your Four Steps and beyond.

CREATIVE VISUALIZATIONS

Match the visualization to the step.

During Step 1: See the face of your dream lover. Imagine his or her nose, chin, and eyes. Linger over details.

During Step 2: See everyone at the office telling you that you look magnificent. Picture the most glamorous person you can think of asking you how you got such a perfect _____.

During Step 3: See yourself at a party filled with incredible people. See yourself doing something you never thought you'd do.

During Step 4: Spend five minutes thinking about a time you were happy by yourself.

A Letter to Your Brain

This is nice to use at any time, but most related to the work you'll be doing in Step 2.

Keep a copy of this letter in your pocket for use when your brain is misbehaving.

Dear Brain:

You know, I love you, I really do. You keep my nervous system working like a well-oiled machine. But sometimes you talk too much. Sometimes you say mean things to me about my body or tell me that I won't be able to do something because it's too difficult. I appreciate your concern for my well-being and value your comments. But right now, I need you to please be quiet.

If what you have to say is really important, I'm sure we can find time to talk about it later.

Right now I'm trying to feel good about myself, so if you can't say anything nice, please don't say anything at all. Of course, if you are able to be supportive and whisper nice things in my ear, then I'd be happy to hear your thoughts on various matters.

Affectionately,
Me

A Final Message from Mr. Alexander

So now you're done, but you're not **really** done, even if you've found your dream partner. A lot of people, including myself, have found love using this system. But I still need a push to get out in the world when I realize I've been hibernating too long. I still need reminders to be kinder to myself. The tools in this book remain useful even after you've found love. Return to them any time you need a refresher.

I want you to have a good relationship, but what I want most for you is a good relationship with yourself. I hope you'll continue to use the ideas in this book until at last you become wholly incorporated into the love energy of the universe and ascend into heaven on a cushion of light.

Curtain Call

I'm the star of my own circus.

Whew! I'm finally done dispensing all that wisdom and can start my own list. "Must be nocturnal ... Must enjoy field mice ..."

I can't wait fo the other shoe to drop!

Good karma is not measured by results. Karma is improved through action. Lucky number: Every number is a lucky number.

Look for my upcom HBO cabaret specia "The Sky Is Fallin Duck!"